Holy Disruptions

"Since God Almighty disrupted us by showing up as Jesus Christ, God with us, savior of the world, we've never been able to resume stability. Since we met Jesus, Prince of peace, we haven't had a moment's peace. Michael Bowe does a wonderful job of reflecting on how divine disruption, otherwise known as Jesus Christ, is nothing less than our salvation. Your days of Advent are sure to be divinely disrupted by Michael's insightful, faithful, devotional insights."

—**WILL WILLIMON**, author of *Changing My Mind: The Neglected Virtue of Ministry*

"As President of Huntsville Bible College, I am honored to commend *Holy Disruptions* by Dr. Michael Bowe. It is a timely and theologically rich devotional that calls the church to pause, reflect, and awaken to the redemptive interruptions of Advent. With pastoral sensitivity and biblical assurance, Dr. Bowe leads readers through the restless terrain of the Advent season with honesty, hope, and a hand pointing towards Christ. His words inspire praise, impart peace, and ignite perseverance. We are proud to count Dr. Bowe among our faculty and celebrate the way this work exemplifies the academic rigor and spiritual integrity we seek to instill at Huntsville Bible College."

—**LYLE LEE**, President, Huntsville Bible College

"I don't usually like distractions. My life is full of them, but that doesn't mean I like them. I like things decent and in order, things that follow the schedule I set. But the disruptions come, and sometimes God is in them. These *Holy Disruptions* from Michael are a tool God will use to disrupt our lives if we allow it. From the first disruption, beginning with peace instead of the traditional hope, these words jump off the page into the midst of our too busy lives. They cry out for us to find time for them. Those who do will find challenges to traditional thinking and believing and assurance that God not only accepts but encourages such things. *Holy Disruptions* is a valuable resource for group or individual reflection. I hope many of us find lots of ways to use it!"

—**Bob Phelps**, Executive Presbyter, North Alabama Presbytery

"Jesus promised that if you knew his teaching, you will be blessed by doing it. Michael's insightful reflections on God's word are inspiring, but the real blessing comes in his suggestions for putting it into practice. This Advent you will be blessed by acting on *Holy Disruptions*. May God use you to be his disruption in another's life."

—**Tom Reynolds**, President, His Way Recovery Center

"*Holy Disruptions* is a timely and hope-filled Advent companion. Michael Bowe invites readers to embrace the unexpected ways God breaks into our lives with grace, challenge, and renewal. A thoughtful and engaging work from a gifted Memphis Theological Seminary alum."

—**Jody Hill**, President, Memphis Theological Seminary

Holy Disruptions

An Advent Devotional for a Restless Church

MICHAEL B. BOWE

RESOURCE *Publications* · Eugene, Oregon

HOLY DISRUPTIONS
An Advent Devotional for a Restless Church

Copyright © 2025 Michael B. Bowe. All rights reserved. Except for brief quotations in critical publications or reviews, no part of this book may be reproduced in any manner without prior written permission from the publisher. Write: Permissions, Wipf and Stock Publishers, 199 W. 8th Ave., Suite 3, Eugene, OR 97401.

Resource Publications
An Imprint of Wipf and Stock Publishers
199 W. 8th Ave., Suite 3
Eugene, OR 97401

www.wipfandstock.com

PAPERBACK ISBN: 979-8-3852-5894-9
HARDCOVER ISBN: 979-8-3852-5895-6
EBOOK ISBN: 979-8-3852-5896-3
VERSION NUMBER 08/14/25

Unless otherwise noted, Scripture quotations are taken from the New Revised Standard Version Updated Edition. Copyright © 2021 National Council of Churches of Christ in the United States of America. Used by permission. All rights reserved worldwide.

To Tammy,
my favorite person and the most life-giving
disruption I never saw coming. I love you.
You have made everything in my life so much better.

To Reanna, Christian, Elijah, and Tyler,
who fill my life with laughter, questions, grace,
and more than a little holy chaos. You each make me
look much better than I really am!

All of you remind me daily that love is loud,
hope is messy, and God's best surprises often
come wrapped in ordinary moments.

This book is for you.

Contents

How to Use This Book | ix
Preface: Disrupting Advent on Purpose | xi
Advent Introduction: A Season We'd Rather Skip | xiii

Week One: Peace | 1
   Day 1: Peace That Wakes Us Up | 3
   Day 2: Remembered by God, Embraced by Peace | 5
   Day 3: Peace After the Storm | 7
   Day 4: An Unshakable Peace | 9
   Day 5: Peace That Unites | 11
   Day 6: Peace That Answers, Not Escapes | 13
   Day 7: Preparing for Peace | 15

Week Two: Joy | 17
   Day 1: When Joy Looks Small | 19
   Day 2: Joy in What God Can Do | 21
   Day 3: Joy in Unlikely Places | 23
   Day 4: Joy That Speaks | 25
   Day 5: Joy in the Waiting | 27
   Day 6: When Joy Isn't Fair | 29
   Day 7: Joy That Shakes Things Up | 31

Week Three: Love | 33
   Day 1: Love That Moves First | 35
   Day 2: Love That Heals the Ache | 37
   Day 3: Love That Flows | 39

    Day 4: Love That Will Not Let Go | 41
    Day 5: Love That Stays Faithful | 43
    Day 6: Love That Names Us | 45
    Day 7: Love That Finishes What It Starts | 47

Week Four: Hope | 49
    Day 1: Hope That Trusts the Promise | 51
    Day 2: Hope That Surprises | 53
    Day 3: Hope That Breaks Through | 55
    Day 4: The Disruption of Belonging | 57
    Day 5: Hope That Moves Us Forward | 59
    Day 6: Hope That Comes Home | 61
    Day 7: Hope That Breaks the Silence | 63

Christmas: The Disruption Fulfilled | 65
    Christmas Eve (Morning): The Disruption We Needed | 67
    Christmas Eve (Nativity): The Disruption
      That Changed Everything | 69
    Christmas Day: The Kind of God Who Came Close | 71

Closing Reflection: Disrupted, Reoriented, Sent | 73

How to Use This Book

THIS DEVOTIONAL IS AN invitation to slow down and make space for reflection during a season that often feels rushed and overstuffed. It's meant to help you think, pray, and engage with God amid real life. Each day's reading is grounded in Scripture, but more than that, it is rooted in the deep themes of Advent—peace, joy, love, and hope.

These devotions follow the Revised Common Lectionary for Year A, based on the Advent season of 2025. Because the calendar shifts from year to year, you may notice that some days don't line up exactly in other years. That's okay. Advent is fluid, and the message of the season doesn't depend on a particular date.

You might be reading this in a different year or not following the lectionary at all. You may be exploring faith for the first time or returning to it after a long season away. Whatever brings you to these pages, you are welcome. The themes of Advent transcend the calendar. They call us to remember, to watch, and to wait.

This book invites you to journey slowly toward Christmas. To see peace not as the absence of conflict but as the presence of God. To find joy that runs deeper than circumstance. To encounter love that moves first. To hold onto hope, even when it flickers faintly.

And at the center of it all is this reminder: God disrupts us—gently, deeply, redemptively. Advent is not about getting everything tidy and in order before Christ arrives. It is about being interrupted by grace. These reflections are meant to stir, to pause,

How to Use This Book

to re-center you around the God who comes, not when we're ready, but when we're most in need.

At the heart of Advent is the stunning truth that God came near. God entered our world, not with spectacle, but with presence. Not above us, but among us. That is the beauty we walk toward—one day at a time.

May these reflections lead you closer to the Christ child, and may every disruption become holy.

Preface

Disrupting Advent on Purpose

ADVENT IS NOT FOR the faint of heart.

These days, Christmas seems to arrive earlier and earlier. Decorations start showing up in stores in September. By October, trees are trimmed in department windows and radio stations are already playing carols. It's tempting to skip over Advent entirely, especially when the music isn't as catchy and the readings feel more like wake-up calls than lullabies. Let's be honest: who really wants to wait anymore?

But if we let Scripture lead the way, we discover that Advent begins, not in stillness, but in disruption. The lectionary texts for the first Sunday of Advent don't whisper. They shout, "Wake up!" Paul writes that salvation is nearer now than when we first believed (Rom 13:11). Jesus warns that the coming of the Son of Man will be unexpected (Matt 24:44). Isaiah dreams of swords beaten into plowshares (Isa 2:4). These are not nostalgic sentiments. They are divine interruptions. Advent, at its heart, is a season that calls us to slow down, pay attention, and prepare, not for a cozy tradition, but for the world-altering arrival of God's reign.

This devotional was born out of a restless kind of hope. As a pastor, I've watched congregations move through December overwhelmed by busyness, distracted by sentimentality, or numbed by loss. I've also seen what happens when we allow the texts of Advent to do what they were meant to do: disrupt, awaken, and remake us.

Preface

Each entry in this book follows the daily lectionary readings, drawing together the Psalms, Prophets, Gospels, and Epistles into a movement through the themes of peace, joy, love, and hope. These devotions don't seek to explain Scripture as much as to enter it, to sit with the tension, wrestle with the promise, and wait with holy discomfort. They are not written to check a devotional box. They are written to walk with you in a season that too often gets lost beneath glitter and noise.

Real peace is not the absence of conflict. It is the presence of justice. Real joy is not a seasonal mood. It is the fruit of longing and grace. Real love does not wait its turn or play it safe. It breaks in, it risks, it restores. And real hope is not optimism or wishful thinking. It is defiant trust in God. Each week includes a brief introduction to guide your heart through the upcoming readings, followed by daily reflections grounded in Scripture. A short prayer closes each day, creating space for honesty, hope, and expectation. These devotions are short enough to accompany a morning routine and deep enough to stir something lasting.

If you're looking for a guide through the familiar rhythms of December, this may not be the book for you. But if you're hungry for more, if you're willing to be disrupted by something holier than sentiment, then I invite you to linger here.

Come, Lord Jesus. Disrupt us with peace. Wake us with joy. Break in with love. And let us never be the same.

Dr. Michael Bowe
Pastor, Faith Presbyterian Church
Huntsville, Alabama

Advent Introduction
A Season We'd Rather Skip

ADVENT IS NOT EVERYONE'S favorite season. It's quieter, slower, less flashy than what comes after. The hymns don't sparkle like the Christmas carols, and the waiting can feel more like wandering. A lot of people skip over Advent entirely, jumping straight into the bright lights and bold choruses of Christmas. And honestly, who can blame them? We don't like waiting. We like instant joy, not patient hope. We like celebration, not preparation.

But Advent offers something we can't find anywhere else in the church calendar: honest expectation. It meets us in the dark and doesn't rush us through it. It gives us space to name what's not right in the world, or in us. It invites us to long for what we still don't yet see.

We live in an age of now. Advent says, Not yet. We live in a culture that demands answers. Advent whispers, Wait. We want Christmas, and we want it today. Advent says, Let God come in God's time.

This season isn't about pretending everything is okay. It's about learning to hope even when it's not. It's about practicing trust in a world full of noise and fear. It's about holding onto the promise that God is not done yet—and neither are we.

So if you're feeling weary, disoriented, or just plain restless, you're not alone. That's where Advent begins. Not in certainty or cheerfulness, but in a holy kind of unrest. And it just might be the disruption we need.

WEEK ONE

Peace

CHRISTMAS SHOWS UP EARLY these days. By September, the store shelves are already filled with garlands and glitter. Trees go up before the Thanksgiving leftovers are cold. The carols play on a loop. And in all the noise and sparkle, the season tries to convince us that peace looks like a cozy home, a warm drink, and a perfect photo.

But Advent tells a different story.

Advent begins with urgency. The Scriptures for this week do not sing us to sleep; they shake us awake. Paul writes to the Romans, "It is now the moment for you to wake from sleep" (13:11). Jesus warns his followers to stay alert, because they do not know the hour of his return (Matt 24:44). Isaiah calls the nations to beat their swords into plowshares and to learn war no more (Isa 2:4). None of these images are passive or quiet. They do not belong on a Hallmark card.

The truth is, we often want peace without change. We long for comfort more than transformation. But real peace does not come by pretending everything is fine. It comes when justice is done, when the low are lifted up, when old weapons are laid aside, and when lives are reordered around God's promises. Advent peace is not the absence of conflict. It is the presence of God in the middle of a world still groaning. It disrupts the patterns we have learned to live with. It asks us to stop settling. It invites us to wait

Week One: Peace

for something better, not by doing nothing, but by living now as though the light is already rising.

This week, we begin by watching and listening. We learn to tell the difference between peace that numbs and peace that heals. We do not rush to Christmas. We stay with the prophets and the warnings and the strange announcements of something new. Because when peace finally arrives, we want to be ready to recognize it.

Day 1

Peace That Wakes Us Up

Texts: Isaiah 2:1–5; Psalm 122;
Romans 13:11–14; Matthew 24:36–44

MANY CHURCHES, ON CHRISTMAS Eve, hold a Lessons and Carols service. Traditionally, the evening ends in near darkness, with a sanctuary full of flickering candles and the gentle sound of "Silent Night" rising from the pews. It's a beautiful moment of stillness, memory, and light. But the season that leads us there begins in a very different key.

Advent opens, not with calm or comfort, but with a startling call to attention. Paul writes to the Roman church with urgency: "Now is the moment to wake from sleep." Jesus, in Matthew's Gospel, says the Son of Man is coming at an unexpected hour, like a thief in the night. Like a thief in the night?!? These are not peaceful words in the soft sense. They are meant to rouse us, to shake us from routine and distraction.

Peace, in Scripture, is rarely sentimental. It is not about escape or comfort. It is about wholeness, justice, and restored relationships. The peace of Advent begins with a disruption. It tells the truth about how much we long for more. It invites us to stop pretending that everything is fine and to start preparing for a kingdom that looks entirely different from what we've known.

Week One: Peace

Isaiah imagines a world where the nations stop warring and instead say, "Come, let us go up to the mountain of the Lord." Swords become plowshares. Weapons become tools for growth. That kind of transformation is not quiet. It upends assumptions and overturns power. It requires us to live as if God's reign is already taking shape in our midst.

Psalm 122 speaks of peace within the city of God. But even that peace is built on movement, on pilgrimage, on the willingness to walk together toward something better.

So we begin here, not at the manger, but at the mountain. Not with lullabies, but with longing. We wait for the One who is coming, and we ask for the courage to let his peace disturb our comfort.

Prayer

God of peace, stir me from sleep. Let your coming interrupt what I've come to accept. Help me walk in your light. Amen.

And may that peace give you courage to live wide awake.

Day 2

Remembered by God, Embraced by Peace

Texts: Psalm 124; Genesis 8:1–19; Romans 6:1–11

WOULDN'T IT BE NICE if everything just always worked out? There was enough money in the bank, no bad news from the doctor, no strained conversations around the dinner table. Unfortunately, that is not the world we live in. Life is rarely predictable, and even more rarely neat. Advent does not ask us to pretend otherwise.

Genesis describes the flood in stark, almost poetic terms. The waters rise. The chaos deepens. The ark drifts on a world undone. That flood story has long stood as a symbol of chaos, of what it feels like when life becomes unmoored. Psalm 124 echoes that feeling: "If the Lord had not been on our side, the flood would have swept us away."

But then, there is a turning point. "God remembered Noah." That is the moment the story changes. Not when the rain stops. Not when the ark touches land. But when divine remembering enters the scene. It is not that God forgot. Rather, Scripture uses memory as a sign of movement. When God remembers, mercy follows.

And that mercy brings more than survival. When the dove finds dry land and the ark settles, what emerges is not simply endurance, it is new creation. Paul picks up that imagery in Romans

Week One: Peace

and names it the promise of baptism. We are not only pulled out of sin. We are raised with Christ to walk in newness of life. Death is not the end. Chaos is not the whole story.

Advent reminds us that God still remembers. The waters do not rise forever. The storms do not get the last word. Whatever has threatened to sweep you away, whether fear, failure, grief, or shame, God sees you. God remembers.

That kind of remembering restores. It renews. It anchors us when everything else feels uncertain. You are not forgotten. You are held.

Prayer

God who remembers, let the floodwaters recede. Help me step out of what has drowned me. Raise me to walk in the newness you promise. Amen.

And may that remembrance give you peace today.

Day 3

Peace After the Storm

Texts: Psalm 124; Genesis 9:1-17;
Hebrews 11:32-40

PSALM 124 SAYS, "IF the Lord had not been on our side, we would have been swallowed alive." Sometimes, life hits really hard. The blow is not metaphorical. It lands. It hurts. And in the aftermath, we're left gasping, wondering if we can get back up.

In the 2006 film *Rocky Balboa*, the aging boxer offers a line that gets quoted often: "It isn't about how hard you can hit, but how hard you can get hit and keep moving forward." It sounds inspiring. But some days, if we're honest, we don't want to move forward, we just want the storm to stop.

We want peace. Relief. Rest from the struggle. But peace doesn't always arrive with a celebration. Sometimes it comes quietly, after the chaos has subsided. That is what happens after the flood. Noah and his family survive the storm, but there is no immediate applause, no divine manual for what to do next.

Instead, God gives a promise. A bow is hung in the sky—not pulled back in wrath but laid down in mercy. The weapon is set aside. God speaks not just to Noah but to all creation. This is not just about one family. It is a universal covenant. Divine peace stretches across the sky and across time.

Week One: Peace

This is the shape of real peace—not the absence of hardship but the presence of mercy. Peace does not always feel like resolution. Often, it feels like a promise holding you together when you're not sure what happens next. Hebrews reminds us of the faithful ones who never received what was promised. They lived in hope, endured suffering, and died waiting. Yet they were not forgotten. They were part of a larger story. So are we.

Advent peace is not a feeling we manufacture. It is a covenant. It holds, even when our strength doesn't. It carries us forward, not because the storm is gone, but because God is present.

Prayer

God of peace, thank you for promises that hold. Teach me to rest in your mercy, even in the aftermath. Amen.

And may that peace steady you wherever the flood has left you.

Day 4

An Unshakable Peace

Texts: Psalm 124; Isaiah 54:1–10; Matthew 24:23–35

PEACE CAN BE HARD to trust, especially when everything feels like it's falling apart. We're not just talking about mild discomfort or seasonal stress. Sometimes, the world feels like it's shaking beneath our feet. Relationships unravel. Systems fail. Illness strikes. Hope wears thin.

Jesus knew this. He told his disciples that people would try to decode signs and disasters, pointing to wars, famines, and false messiahs. It would be tempting to believe that chaos marked the end of the story. But Jesus didn't tell them to panic. He gave them a promise. "Heaven and earth will pass away," he said, "but my words will not pass away."

In other words, when everything else falls, God's word stands. Isaiah 54 echoes that hope with striking tenderness. Speaking to a people who felt abandoned and ashamed, God offers a new vision—not of rejection but of redemption. "Though the mountains may depart and the hills be removed, my steadfast love shall not depart from you," God says, "and my covenant of peace shall not be removed." This is not sentimental poetry. It is a covenant, a deep, durable promise that does not break even under pressure.

Week One: Peace

Psalm 124 brings that promise into personal memory. "If the Lord had not been on our side," the psalmist writes, "we would have been swallowed alive." That line doesn't deny the danger. It names it. The people really were threatened. The floodwaters were real. But they were not abandoned.

That's the kind of peace Advent gives us—not a denial of difficulty but an anchor in the midst of it. A peace that has weathered storms before and will hold again. It is not the absence of fear but the presence of God. And it is stronger than the winds that howl around us.

Prayer

God of the covenant, help me trust your peace when everything else feels shaky. Remind me that your love does not leave, even when the world does. Amen.

And may that peace hold you steady, even when the mountains shift.

Day 5

Peace That Unites

Texts: Psalm 72:1–7, 18–19; Isaiah 4:2–6; Acts 1:12–17, 21–26

SOMETIMES PEACE FEELS BROKEN. After Jesus ascended, the disciples didn't erupt in praise or rush out in power. They retreated to a familiar room, not with confidence—but with questions. What now? What next? Everything had changed again. And though the Scriptures say they were of "one accord," it's hard to believe they weren't also afraid.

So they did the only thing they knew to do: they prayed. Not from a place of clarity, but from a place of anxiety. They prayed, not because everything was right, but because they knew they needed each other—and they needed God. That kind of prayer, born in confusion and spoken in community, is sacred. It reminds us that peace doesn't always come after the storm has passed; sometimes it arrives in the middle of it.

Peace did not fall like a blanket that day. It rose from within their shared waiting. It grew in community. That is often how peace arrives—not as a dramatic fix, but as the quiet strength found in unity. In the absence of easy answers, they chose to remain together, to wait on the Lord side by side. And that made all the difference.

Week One: Peace

Isaiah speaks of a shelter, a canopy of protection for those who remain. It's not flashy or loud—but it's strong. Psalm 72 reminds us that peace comes through justice, through remembering the poor and lifting up the vulnerable. And in Acts, we witness disciples who didn't scatter, but instead leaned into the uncomfortable uncertainty with a spirit of togetherness.

In all three texts, peace is not the absence of conflict but the presence of care. It is God gathering us together when everything feels scattered. It is God whispering, even now, "You're not alone."

Prayer

God of unity, when I feel anxious or unsure, help me to turn to you and to others. Teach me to trust that peace does not depend on having all the answers—but on being held in your presence. Amen.

May you find peace, not in knowing what comes next, but in knowing you are not alone.

Day 6

Peace That Answers, Not Escapes

Texts: Psalm 72:1–7, 18–19; Isaiah 30:19–26; Acts 13:16–25

PEACE ISN'T ALWAYS QUIET. It doesn't always show up wrapped in calm. Sometimes, it comes right in the middle of the noise, the weariness, the mess. Advent doesn't ignore how hard life can be. It names it. And then it promises something more.

Isaiah doesn't offer peace as a fantasy. He writes to a people who have suffered, who made poor choices, who feel the weight of their consequences. But now, he says, "The Lord waits to be gracious to you." God doesn't come with scolding. God comes with healing. There will be bread. There will be light. The wounds will be bound. Peace shows up in real ways.

Psalm 72 echoes that. It's not a song about escaping trouble—it's about confronting it with justice. The king in this psalm defends the poor, delivers the needy, and brings peace that soaks the land like rain. This isn't sentimental. It's systemic. Peace here means things change.

And when Paul preaches in Acts, he roots Jesus in that very kind of story—a story of God stepping in, again and again, to act with mercy when the people fail. The promise of peace stretches back generations. And still, it holds.

Week One: Peace

Advent doesn't ask us to pretend. It asks us to hope. And it reminds us that peace, real peace, doesn't just comfort. It restores.

Prayer

God who binds up wounds, don't let me settle for shallow peace. Let your promises shape my hope and your justice reshape my world. Amen.

And may that peace be real enough to touch what hurts.

Day 7

Preparing for Peace

Texts: Psalm 72:1–7, 18–19;
Isaiah 40:1–11; John 1:19–28

"Comfort, O comfort my people," begins Isaiah's song. It's a word of peace spoken into exhaustion. After exile, after silence, after sorrow, God speaks again. Not with thunder but with comfort. Not with vengeance but with preparation.

Isaiah 40 calls us to make space: to level the hills, lift the valleys, clear the way. But this isn't about road construction. It's about the heart. Peace does not come to crowded, hardened places. It comes where space has been made.

And that's the hard part. We want peace to just show up and fix things, to quiet the noise and resolve the tension without requiring anything from us. But Isaiah reminds us that the path of peace is a participatory one. We prepare the way. We take the first faithful steps, even when the road is still rough and the landscape uneven. We begin clearing space in our lives and our world for what God will soon do.

John the Baptist knew this. When asked who he was, he didn't reach for prestige. He didn't say he was a prophet or a priest. He said, "I am the voice." Not the light. Not the messiah. Just the voice crying out, Make room. He understood that peace begins

Week One: Peace

not with arrival but with preparation. Before Christ comes in glory, there must be space for him in our hearts, in our homes, and in our hopes.

Psalm 72 reminds us what that peace will look like. It will bring justice, righteousness, and flourishing. But even then, it starts as a prayer: "Give the king your justice, O God." It begins with longing, with desire, with trust that God will act in mercy and power.

Advent peace may not come instantly. But it is coming. And we prepare, not with answers, but with open hands and cleared paths.

Prayer

God of peace, help me make space. Clear what is cluttered in me. Open what is closed. Prepare in me a way for your comfort to come. Amen.

And may the peace you prepare for meet you in the waiting.

WEEK TWO

Joy

JOY IS OFTEN MISUNDERSTOOD. We confuse it with happiness or assume it must always feel light, bubbly, or easy. But biblical joy has roots deeper than mood. It is not a fleeting emotion. It is a defiant, holy confidence that God is still at work even when circumstances suggest otherwise.

Advent joy begins in strange places. It comes in the wilderness, where paths are made straight. It breaks into barrenness and exile. It visits shepherds working night shifts and prophets wearing camel hair. It does not wait for the world to be polished or perfect. It shows up anyway.

In this season, joy interrupts the expected. It disrupts despair and whispers hope into long silences. It invites us to imagine a world remade by God's love. But that invitation is not sentimental. Joy calls us to prepare. To turn. To make room. To live as though God's kingdom is near.

The joy of Advent is not a distraction from reality. It is the promise that something more is coming. A joy that cannot be taken, because it does not depend on what we can see.

This week, may we open our hearts to that kind of joy. The joy that sings while we wait, the joy that trusts while we prepare, the joy that changes us from the inside out.

WEEK TWO

Day 1

When Joy Looks Small

Texts: Isaiah 11:1-10; Psalm 72:1-7, 18-19;
Romans 15:4-13; Matthew 3:1-12

WHEN I WAS YOUNGER, I loved watching Christmas parades. I waited the whole time just to see Santa at the end. That moment brought joy to me as a child, bright, loud, full of energy. But as I've grown older, I've learned that joy doesn't always arrive like a parade. Sometimes it comes quietly, like a green shoot breaking through dry ground.

Isaiah says, "A shoot shall come out from the stump of Jesse." Not a tall tree, not a sudden miracle, but something small. The tree is cut down, yet life begins again. This is joy that rises from what seemed finished. It is the quiet resilience of God's promises, taking root in places that looked barren. That single shoot holds the hope of restoration, not just for Israel, but for all creation. The wolf and the lamb, the calf and the lion, all dwell together in peace because a child leads them. This joy is not just personal, it is cosmic, stretching from the roots of David's line to the renewal of the earth.

Romans reminds us that this joy is born from Scripture and held by the Spirit. It is not a cheap optimism, but a deep trust that God is faithful to what has been written and spoken. Paul calls us to endure and to live in harmony, so that "with one voice" we may

Week Two: Joy

glorify the God of hope. Joy, in this sense, is communal. It lifts others with it.

Psalm 72 gives texture to what God's kingdom looks like when that joy begins to take hold. It pictures a ruler who delivers the needy, defends the poor, and brings justice to the oppressed. Joy doesn't erupt from personal gain or fleeting pleasures, but from a world where the vulnerable are lifted up and righteousness flows like fresh rain on new grass.

When John the Baptist cries out in the wilderness, the setting doesn't feel joyful—but the message carries joy all the same. Something new is coming. The world is about to change.

Advent joy doesn't always shine. Sometimes it sprouts. And sometimes, that is more than enough.

Prayer

God of joy, thank you for small beginnings. Teach me to notice joy in quiet places, and to trust that your goodness is still growing. Amen.

And may that joy grow in you, one green shoot at a time.

Day 2

Joy in What God Can Do

Texts: Psalm 21; Isaiah 24:1–16a; 1 Thessalonians 4:1–12

SOMETIMES JOY IS HARD to find. Isaiah paints a haunting picture—earth languishing, joy withering, song silenced. The world reels under the weight of brokenness. And yet, right in the middle of that vision, a song begins: "They lift up their voices, they sing for joy." It is not because things are perfect. It's not because sorrow is absent. It's because, even amid devastation, God's glory still shines.

Joy, in the biblical witness, is not rooted in circumstance. It is not the reward for comfort or ease. It is the response of faith in a God who remains good even when the world groans. As Isaiah says, "From the ends of the earth we hear songs of praise, of glory to the Righteous One."

Psalm 21 echoes this same defiant joy. The king rejoices not in military power but in God's strength. The psalm is full of confidence, not because the threats are gone, but because God's steadfast love holds firm. This is not triumphalism; it is trust.

In 1 Thessalonians, Paul turns his attention to ordinary, faithful life. There's no hint of escapism or fantasy. He urges believers to "aspire to live quietly, to mind your own affairs, and to work with your hands." Sometimes joy doesn't look like celebration. It looks like stability. It looks like holiness. It looks like continuing in love for one another, even when things feel unstable.

Advent joy doesn't ignore the world's pain. It sings in the midst of it. It holds fast to God's righteousness, lives faithfully in community, and trusts that, even in shaking, we are held.

Prayer

God of joy and endurance, help me to sing when the world feels silent. Give me joy that is rooted in your presence, not in perfect conditions. Let me live quietly, love faithfully, and trust your goodness today. Amen.

And may that joy hold you when everything else feels uncertain.

Day 3

Joy in Unlikely Places

Texts: Psalm 21; Isaiah 41:14–20; Romans 15:14–21

GOD DOESN'T ALWAYS START with the strong. In Isaiah 41, God calls Israel, not a warrior or a hero, but a "worm"—fragile, insignificant, easily overlooked. It's not the title anyone would want on a résumé. And yet, this is where the promise lands. "Do not fear, I will help you," God says. Joy does not come from status or strength, but from divine presence. The wilderness will become a garden, the barren heights will flow with rivers, and what once felt lifeless will teem with beauty. That is what God does. Not because we are mighty but because God is.

Psalm 21 captures a similar moment, but from the other side of deliverance. The king rejoices, not in his own victory, but in the strength of the Lord. "You meet him with rich blessings," the psalmist sings. The joy here is not self-congratulatory. It is worshipful. It is joy that remembers where the strength came from and who carried the day.

Paul knew this kind of joy well. In Romans 15, he reflects on his ministry not with self-praise but humility. "I will not venture to speak of anything except what Christ has accomplished through me." He boasts not in his credentials but in what God has done. His joy is to be a witness, a servant, a messenger of grace.

Week Two: Joy

Advent joy, then, is not about impressiveness. It does not rise from ambition or recognition. It is born in places we often overlook—quiet faithfulness, dry deserts, weary hearts that have stopped trying to earn joy and are instead learning to receive it.

This is the joy of Advent: God doing new things in unlikely places, with unlikely people. The kind of joy that sprouts in silence and breaks open what we thought was barren.

Prayer

God of joy, use what is small in me. Let your strength shine through my weakness. Grow joy in me that comes not from what I can do but from what you are doing. Amen.

And may that joy lead you to trust what God can do through you.

Day 4

Joy That Speaks

Texts: Psalm 21; Genesis 15:1-18;
Matthew 12:33-37

SOMETIMES JOY LOOKS LIKE confidence. Other times, it looks like a question followed by quiet trust. God tells Abram, "Do not be afraid." But Abram is afraid. He is aging, childless, and unsure how God's promises will unfold. He doesn't hide his fear—he names it. "What will you give me?" he asks. And yet, even in his questioning, he believes. That belief is not mere optimism; it's a courageous trust in a God who speaks into barrenness. It is that trust, Scripture tells us, that is reckoned to him as righteousness. Joy begins not in having the answer but in being willing to trust the One who does.

Psalm 21 echoes what happens when that trust matures. The psalmist writes, "The king rejoices in your strength, O Lord." This is not the celebration of a self-made ruler. It is the joy of someone who knows where their strength comes from. The king's delight is not in his own power but in God's faithfulness, in the blessings poured out from beyond him. This is joy that arises from a life anchored in divine reliability.

In Matthew 12, Jesus makes a profound connection between heart and speech. "Out of the abundance of the heart the mouth speaks." What fills us will eventually overflow. If bitterness takes

25

Week Two: Joy

root, it will surface. But so will joy, if we let God plant it there. Our words carry weight, not just for others, but as reflections of our inner world. They reveal what we trust, what we fear, and what we're still hoping for.

Advent joy is not always exuberant. It doesn't always arrive with trumpets or fanfare. Sometimes it begins as a seed planted in uncertainty, grows slowly in trust, and finally gives rise to speech—not loud but true. Joy often whispers before it sings. And when it speaks, it does so with healing, gratitude, and grace.

Prayer

God of covenant and promise, shape my heart so that my words carry joy. Teach me to trust you, even when I do not yet see. Amen.

And may your joy speak for you, even before you realize it is there.

Day 5

Joy in the Waiting

Texts: Psalm 146:5–10; Ruth 1:6–18; 2 Peter 3:1–10

JOY IS NOT ALWAYS loud. Sometimes it stays with someone through quiet, painful faithfulness. Ruth is one of my favorite books. I had to read it in seminary, slowly, because we read it in Hebrew. Line by line, the story unfolded—and it changed me. It's not just a love story. It's a story of loss, loyalty, and unexpected joy. It is about two women walking back to Bethlehem, not because they know what will happen, but because they believe something might.

Naomi had lost everything. Ruth had every reason to leave. But something in her held on. "Where you go, I will go." Ruth's words are not shouted in triumph. They are whispered in the wilderness, a vow made in the ruins of hope. She has no guarantees, no safety net. Yet she chooses presence over escape. And somehow, joy still lives there—not in outcomes but in faithfulness.

Psalm 146 says the Lord lifts up those who are bowed down, gives food to the hungry, and watches over the stranger. These are not miracles of spectacle. They are slow joys. Faithful joys. They take time, but they always come. This is the kind of God who acts—not always dramatically but always dependably. The joy here is not about abundance; it is about provision. Not about escape, but presence.

Week Two: Joy

Second Peter speaks to the tension we know too well—the feeling that God's promises are delayed. The community wondered when Christ would return, why justice hadn't yet come. But Peter reminds them that God's time is not ours. "With the Lord, one day is like a thousand years." What feels slow is often mercy. What feels quiet is still unfolding. God's slowness is not forgetfulness but patience. And patience, too, is a kind of joy.

Advent joy is not only for the end of the story. It is for the road too. It lives in loyalty. It survives in waiting. It keeps walking even when there is no map. And sometimes, it begins right when we think the story is over.

Prayer

God who waits with us, give me joy that lasts longer than feelings. Help me trust your timing and let your faithfulness be enough for today. Amen.

And may that joy stay close, even when everything else seems far away.

Day 6

When Joy Isn't Fair

Texts: Psalm 146:5–10; Ruth 4:13–17; 2 Peter 3:11–18

RUTH'S STORY ENDS WITH joy, but not the uncomplicated kind. She gives birth to a son, but the women of the village name him. Naomi holds the child. The community proclaims joy over Naomi's restoration, and Ruth—the one who made it all possible—quietly disappears from the spotlight.

There is joy in this moment. A new child. A future secured. A legacy that will lead to David, and eventually to Christ. But the joy comes at a cost. Ruth's name is barely mentioned again. Her identity, her voice, her body, all offered up for a story that moves on without her. The text honors her, but it does not center on her.

Many of us know this kind of joy. The kind that comes after sacrifice. The kind that costs something of ourselves. The kind that doesn't always leave room for our own celebration. It is real joy, but it is complicated.

Psalm 146 reminds us that God sees what others miss. God watches over the stranger, upholds the orphan, and lifts those bowed down. Ruth may disappear from the page, but she does not vanish from God's sight. Her joy is known, even if unspoken.

Week Two: Joy

Second Peter reminds us that this in-between time—between promise and fulfillment—is a space for holy living. We are invited not just to wait but to lean into the work of faith, trusting that the story is not over. God's justice remembers what others overlook. God's joy includes those who are left out of the spotlight.

Advent joy isn't always loud or fair or symmetrical. Sometimes, it is the kind of joy that emerges when you give yourself away and find that God still sees you.

Prayer

God of the overlooked, thank you for remembering those who disappear from the center of the story. Let joy rise even in places where we feel unseen. Amen.

And may that joy find you, even when it does not feel fair.

Day 7

Joy That Shakes Things Up

Texts: Psalm 146:5–10; 1 Samuel 2:1–8; Luke 3:1–18

I LOVE A GOOD love song. I can't sing worth a lick, but I love music that moves me. I love lyrics that say something honest, something raw, songs that don't just entertain but tell the truth.

Hannah's song in 1 Samuel is not a lullaby. It is a cry of joy, but not the gentle kind. This is joy that overturns the world. "The bows of the mighty are broken," she says, "but the feeble gird on strength." That is not sentiment, it's revolution. It is joy that rises when the powerless are lifted up, when the forgotten are remembered, when the world's order is turned on its head. It isn't polite or safe. It is holy and disruptive.

Psalm 146 sings in harmony. God feeds the hungry, frees prisoners, lifts up the lowly, and brings justice to the oppressed. This is good news, but it is not quiet news. Joy like that doesn't hum in the background, it shakes the system. Sometimes it comes more like a trumpet blast than a whisper.

John the Baptist picks up that rhythm in Luke. His words are sharp. He tells people to repent, to bear fruit, to wake up. He names injustice. He exposes complacency. He invites change. And still, people come. They come because something in them knows that joy begins in disruption. That real joy doesn't coddle us, it calls us to something deeper.

Advent joy does not keep the world as it is. It does not wait politely at the margins. It moves in, tells the truth, clears the way, and makes room for something new. It is not rooted in guilt but in grace. It doesn't shame us into change—it invites us, stirs us, calls us. Because joy is coming. And we do not want to miss it.

Prayer

God of holy disruption, give me the courage to welcome the joy that changes things. Let my heart be soft enough to be shaped by your truth. Amen.

And may that joy stir something new in you, even today.

WEEK THREE

Love

We talk a lot about love in December. It's in the cards we send, the songs on the radio, and the movies on TV. But Advent love isn't just cozy or sentimental. It is disruptive, embodied, and persistent. It moves toward people who don't deserve it and into places that don't expect it.

This season reminds us that love does not begin with us. As 1 John says, "We love because he first loved us." Advent love doesn't wait for the right moment or the perfect mood. It arrives early and unexpectedly, much like Christ himself, born to a world too crowded to make room.

God's love shows up in the dark. It comes while we are still hurting, still waiting, still unsure. It speaks to wandering prophets and expectant mothers, to confused disciples and chaotic crowds. In Scripture, love is not just a feeling. It is a movement. It is a promise. It is a person.

Love always takes a risk. It opens us to joy and to sorrow, to healing and to heartbreak. But if Advent teaches us anything, it is that real love always moves first. It crosses boundaries, breaks silence, and makes a way where there was none.

Day 1

Love That Moves First

Texts: Isaiah 35:1–10; Luke 1:46b–55;
James 5:7–10; Matthew 11:2–11

IT TOOK ME TEN years to win my wife's heart. There were moments I thought I should give up and move on. But I am so glad I didn't. Waiting was hard, but love made the first move long before anything looked certain.

Love doesn't wait for perfect timing. Love steps in first. John the Baptist sits in prison, wondering if he got it wrong. "Are you the one?" he asks Jesus. And Jesus doesn't answer with a lecture. He answers with lives. "The blind receive sight, the lame walk, the lepers are cleansed, the deaf hear." Love is already at work, even when we're not sure.

That's what Advent teaches us: God's love doesn't arrive with fanfare. It grows quietly in wombs, in wildernesses, in the silence of longing hearts. Isaiah 35 gives us a vision: deserts blooming, knees strengthened, fears stilled. This is the poetry of divine restoration. God's love doesn't just soothe our hearts. It reorders creation.

James tells us to wait, but like a farmer: alert, hopeful, expectant. Love is already working beneath the surface. We don't control the timing, but we can trust the process. The psalmist sings that

Week Three: Love

the Lord lifts the lowly, upends injustice, and watches over the vulnerable. God's love is not theory. It is action.

Mary's song, the Magnificat, is all love in motion. She rejoices not because life is easy but because God is faithful. The hungry are filled. The proud are brought low. She sings because love has broken in—and she believes it will keep doing so.

Advent love is not cautious. It does not wait politely. It breaks in where the world least expects it.

Prayer

God of steadfast love, thank you for moving toward us before we ever moved toward you. Let your love break into my assumptions, my fears, and my waiting. Amen.

And may that love surprise you, even before you are ready for it.

Day 2

Love That Heals the Ache

Texts: Psalm 42; Isaiah 29:17–24; Acts 5:12–16

"Why are you cast down, O my soul?" That is not a question of doubt. It is a question asked in the dark, by someone who still believes the light will come. Psalm 42 names something deep. Love does not always feel close. There are seasons when God feels distant, when the ache in our chest feels louder than any promise. Advent gives us space to name that ache and to wait for the God who meets us in it. The psalmist's voice is not theoretical—it is personal, raw, and desperate: "My tears have been my food day and night." This is grief that lingers, that consumes. It is, as I once preached, the kind of ache that feels like a question echoing from deep inside: Where is your God?

That's the thing about grief—it doesn't always ask for answers. It asks for presence. And the astonishing thing about this psalm is that even in the questioning, there is a refrain of hope: "Hope in God, for I shall again praise him, my salvation and my God." This is faith that has learned to walk through the cave, not avoid it. This is love that listens in the silence and does not rush past pain.

Isaiah joins the chorus, declaring that the barren will bloom, the deaf will hear, and the humble will rejoice in the Lord. God's love rewrites what we assumed was permanent—grief, desolation, silence. It is not poetic optimism; it is the reality of divine presence in unexpected places. In the darkest caves of our souls, God still whispers.

And in Acts, we glimpse that love in power. People bring their brokenness close, hoping even Peter's shadow might bring healing. That is the cry of a world that aches—and believes. And God answers. Not always in spectacle, but sometimes in shadow. Even there, love moves.

Advent love does not pretend the pain isn't real. It moves toward it. It listens. It heals. Slowly, sometimes. Suddenly, at other times. But always with compassion.

Prayer

God of mercy, when my soul is cast down, help me remember your love. Let my thirst for you be met with your healing presence. Amen.

And may that love hold you gently in the waiting and the wondering.

Day 3

Love That Flows

Texts: Psalm 42; Ezekiel 47:1–12; Jude 1:17–25

A LOT OF PEOPLE think they are in love when, in reality, they are in limerence. Limerence is an intense emotional high, often mistaken for romantic love. It can last anywhere from three months to three years. But limerence is not real love.

Real love is more. It can be romantic, but it is also tenacious. It is sustaining. It holds on through silence, frustration, and disappointment. Real love does not burn out when the feelings fade. It flows.

Psalm 42 says, "As a deer longs for flowing streams, so my soul longs for you, O God." That is not just a metaphor for spiritual inspiration. It is a cry from someone who is parched and barely holding on. This is not about mountaintop experiences. It is about surviving in the valley. Love, in this psalm, is not abstract. It is what keeps a person alive.

Ezekiel's vision mirrors that kind of hope. He sees water trickling from the temple threshold, at first a stream, then a river no one can cross. Wherever the water goes, life springs up. Trees bear fruit every month. Saltwater becomes fresh. What seemed dead is renewed. This is what God's presence does. This is what real love does—it restores what we thought was gone for good.

Week Three: Love

Jude urges us to remain in the love of God. That love is not a passing emotion. It is a current. It invites us in. It carries us forward. It sustains us when we cannot go on by ourselves. Jude reminds us that love is not earned; it is mercy that holds us and presents us, faultless, before God's glory with great joy.

Advent love is not a moment. It is not a feeling. It flows with grace, with life, and with quiet power.

Prayer

God of steady love, save me from settling for something shallow. Let your love flow through the dry places in me. Let it heal, sustain, and renew. Amen.

And may that love carry you, long after the feelings fade.

Day 4

Love That Will Not Let Go

Texts: Psalm 42; Zechariah 8:1–17; Matthew 8:14–17, 28–34

LOVE IS RISKY. REAL love leaves you vulnerable. It can open you up like a fresh wound, and sometimes the other person does not bring ointment. They bring salt.

But real love does not stay at a safe distance. Real love takes risks. Real love moves close. It is willing to enter into pain, to carry burdens that are not its own. It is willing to hope even when disappointment is likely, and to remain present long enough for healing to begin. It listens when silence would be easier. It shows up when walking away would be more convenient. It opens the door, even when fear says to keep it shut.

In Zechariah, God speaks with fierce affection. "I am zealous for Zion with great zeal." This is not soft or sentimental. It is a love that rebuilds ruined places and demands truth, justice, and peace. God's love is not passive; it is active. It refuses to leave things as they are. It rebuilds streets where children can play again. It restores the dignity of those who were once forgotten. It moves into brokenness, not with a sigh of resignation, but with a holy resolve to heal.

Week Three: Love

Psalm 42 gives us the voice of someone who feels the absence of love. "Why are you cast down, O my soul?" The ache is real. But even that ache is shaped by love, because it longs for what once was and still hopes for what could be. This is not despair speaking. It is a soul still tethered to God, still remembering worship, still reaching for the One who feels far away. The longing itself is evidence of love that has not died. When the psalmist thirsts for God like a deer panting for water, it is not poetic flourish. It is survival. Real love doesn't always sing, it sometimes sobs.

In Matthew, Jesus moves toward the sick, toward the demon-possessed, and toward the ones everyone else avoids. He does not love from a distance. He touches. He heals. He enters their chaos and brings peace. He steps into a fevered room, a tormented mind, a haunted graveyard. And he brings healing, not just through miracles, but through nearness. His love is not afraid of mess or madness. His love confronts it, stands firm in it, and speaks peace over it.

Advent love is not about comfort. It is about presence. It comes close, even when it costs everything. It remains when others leave. It risks everything to make things whole.

Prayer

God of courageous love, thank you for drawing near to broken places. Give me the courage to love with risk, to draw near when I would rather walk away. Amen.

And may that love meet you in the risk and stay with you through the pain.

Day 5

Love That Stays Faithful

Texts: Psalm 80:1–7, 17–19; 2 Samuel 7:1–17; Galatians 3:23–29

THERE ARE TIMES WHEN God feels far away. During Advent, we often picture God as tender and near—coming to us as a baby. But even then, God's promises can feel distant, especially when the waiting drags on. Psalm 80 gives voice to that ache. It is the cry of a people worn thin: "Restore us, O God. Let your face shine, that we may be saved." There is longing in their words—but also faith. The kind of faith that keeps reaching, even when it feels like God has gone quiet.

David, too, is at a place of rest. He wants to build something lasting for God—a house, a legacy, a permanent sign of his devotion. But God flips the script. God doesn't ask David to build. Instead, God promises to build something for David. "I will raise up your offspring . . . I will establish the throne of his kingdom forever." Love speaks, not with demands, but with faithfulness. It is covenant, not contract. And God keeps covenant, even when people forget.

In Galatians, Paul says the law was like a guardian, holding us until something better arrived. That "better" is Christ, and in him we are all children of God. That kind of love refuses to divide. It

Week Three: Love

does not care about Jew or Greek, slave or free, male or female. It sees beyond status and distinction. It binds us together.

Advent love is not about sentiment. It is about faithfulness—God's faithfulness. It reminds us that, even in the waiting, even in the weariness, God is building something that will last. Something not made with hands but with love that refuses to let go.

Prayer

Faithful God, when I grow tired of waiting, remind me of your promise. Let your love restore what is weary in me. Let your covenant keep me, even when I can't keep it myself. Amen.

And may that love hold you, even when you don't know how to hold on.

Day 6

Love That Names Us

Texts: Psalm 80:1-7, 17-19;
2 Samuel 7:18-22; Galatians 4:1-7

THERE IS SOMETHING POWERFUL about being named. Not just called by a label, but recognized. Claimed. Beloved. Dale Carnegie, in his classic book *How to Win Friends and Influence People*, once noted that a person's name is to that person the sweetest sound in any language. Why? Because naming is about dignity. It says you are seen, remembered, valued. Scripture tells the story of a God who does not love from a distance but enters our story and gives us a name.

God calls people by name—Abraham, Moses, Mary—not because God forgets but because naming is a form of knowing. It is how love becomes personal. God names us not as a crowd but as individuals. Not just as workers or worshipers but as children. In Christ, we are no longer strangers or slaves but beloved sons and daughters.

David, in 2 Samuel 7, responds to God's overwhelming promise with humility: "Who am I, O Lord God, and what is my house, that you have brought me thus far?" He knows he hasn't earned this love. He knows God knows who he is, flaws and all. Yet God chooses him anyway. God makes a covenant, not because David deserves it, but because God's love is faithful.

Psalm 80 echoes the longing to be remembered. "Restore us, O God," the psalmist cries again and again. It is a plea from those who feel cut off. Forgotten. Unnamed. But even in that cry is hope. A belief that God still hears. That God still sees. That God still calls.

Paul's words in Galatians take that hope further. We are no longer under a guardian, he says, but full heirs. Through Christ, we are adopted. Named. Claimed. God no longer sees us through the lens of status or separation. We are all one. And we are all known.

Advent love is not a vague sentiment. It is covenantal. It reaches into silence and draws us out by name. Even when we're not sure we belong, God calls us anyway.

Prayer

God who names and claims me, when I feel forgotten, remind me that I belong to you. Let your love be louder than my fear. Let your promise hold me steady. Amen.

And may that love call you by name, even when you feel invisible.

Day 7

Love That Finishes What It Starts

Texts: Psalm 80:1–7, 17–19; 2 Samuel 7:23–29; John 3:31–36

WE'VE ALL SEEN IT—what some call the "honeymoon phase." It's emotional, intense, and often confused with love. Psychologists have a word for it: limerence. It's that early rush of infatuation that feels unstoppable. But over time, feelings fade. The glow dims. And we're left with a question: Was it love, or just the thrill of being seen?

God's love is not like limerence. It doesn't wear off. It doesn't waver when things get hard. The love of God is covenantal. It starts with grace and ends with redemption. It is not emotional whimsy but faithful pursuit.

David sees this in 2 Samuel 7. After being promised an everlasting legacy, he doesn't boast—he prays. "Who am I, O Lord God?" he says. David remembers God's past faithfulness and believes that God will finish what was started. Not because of David's merit, but because of God's mercy.

Psalm 80 echoes this trust. "Restore us, O God . . . let your face shine." The people are tired. The promises feel far away. But they keep asking. They keep believing. Because they know God's love is not a passing phase. It stays. It saves.

Week Three: Love

In John's Gospel, we are reminded why: Jesus is not just a messenger. He is the fulfillment. "The one who comes from above is above all." In him, the love of God takes shape—real, lasting, complete.

Advent love is not just something we feel for a season. It is something that carries us to the end. It does not sparkle and fade. It shines through the shadows and stays until the promise is fulfilled.

Prayer

Faithful God, when the glow wears off and the waiting feels long, remind me that your love endures. Complete the good work you have begun in me. Amen.

And may that love outlast every doubt and carry you through every season.

WEEK FOUR

Hope

ADVENT ENDS WHERE IT began, not with certainty, but with promise. Hope, in the biblical sense, is not wishful thinking. It is a steady, stubborn trust that what God has said will come to pass, even if we cannot yet see it. But, hope can be hard to hold onto. It gets mistaken for optimism, confused with denial, or reduced to wishful thinking. But biblical hope is none of those things. It is defiant. It trusts in what God has promised, even when everything else says otherwise.

Advent hope doesn't ignore the darkness; it speaks into it. It shows up in prison cells and deserts, in grieving hearts and silent nights. It whispers when the world is loud and waits when the world rushes. Hope doesn't come with certainty. It comes with trust.

The hope of Advent is not rooted in our circumstances but in God's character. It holds space for the not-yet, for the tension between promise and fulfillment. It believes that, even now, God is still moving. Still healing. Still coming.

Hope doesn't always feel triumphant. Sometimes it looks like a remnant, a whisper, a flicker. But even then, it's enough. Because the God who came once is coming again. And that is our real hope!

Day 1

Hope That Trusts the Promise

Texts: Isaiah 7:10-16; Psalm 80:1-7, 17-19;
Romans 1:1-7; Matthew 1:18-25

Hope doesn't always look confident, because it isn't. Sometimes it looks like fear, or hesitation, or showing up even when you'd rather run away. I remember when my youngest son played baseball. He was afraid of the ball, which made it all the more surprising when the coach put him at catcher. That meant crouching behind the plate while fast pitches came hurling toward him. He was nervous, tense, even scared—but he suited up, got in position, and hoped he'd be okay. He didn't have confidence, but he had enough trust to stay in the game. That's what real hope looks like.

That's also where we meet Joseph in Matthew's Gospel. He has every reason to back out. The story he's being asked to believe defies logic and upends tradition. And yet, God speaks and Joseph stays.

Isaiah's prophecy to Ahaz came during a time of great fear. The people of Judah were under threat, and the king wanted security. But God offered something better: a sign. "The young woman is with child," Isaiah said, "and shall bear a son, and shall name him Immanuel." God with us. Not just in theory, but in the middle

Week Four: Hope

of threat and uncertainty. Real hope never arrives in a vacuum. It comes when we need it most.

Psalm 80 is a communal cry: "Restore us, O God . . . let your face shine, that we may be saved." That cry is not weakness. It's faith. It's the kind of hope that keeps asking, even in the waiting.

In Romans, Paul calls himself a servant, set apart for the gospel, chosen to carry a message rooted in promise. That's what hope really is: trust that God keeps promises. Even when the road is uncertain. Even when the sign is a baby. Even when what we hoped for comes in a different form than we expected.

Advent begins not with certainty but with a whisper of promise. And that's more than enough.

Prayer

God of the promise, teach me to hope when I cannot see the way forward. Let your word speak louder than my fear, and your presence outshine the dark. Amen.

And may that hope carry you when everything else feels unclear.

Day 2

Hope That Surprises

Texts: 1 Samuel 2:1–10; Genesis 17:15–22; Galatians 4:8–20

I WAS NINETEEN WHEN my oldest daughter was born. I was terrified. My life mirrored that country song by Kenny Chesney, "There Goes My Life." I didn't feel ready. I didn't feel wise or steady. All I felt was fear. But even then, something else began to stir, something small and stubborn. Looking back, I would call it hope.

Hope doesn't always arrive with fireworks or clarity. Sometimes, it sneaks in through laughter, disbelief, or the weariness of waiting. That was true for Abraham. When God promised a son through Sarah, Abraham laughed. Maybe it was joy. Maybe it was mockery. Most likely it was disbelief. The promise sounded absurd—too far-fetched to be taken seriously. "Can Sarah, who is ninety years old, bear a child?" But God didn't scold the laughter. Instead, God doubled down on the promise.

But God doesn't operate by probability. God makes promises that reshape what we thought was possible. In Abraham and Sarah's case, the promise of Isaac was more than a personal joy. It was the beginning of a covenant people. Hope may start small, but it grows into something lasting.

Week Four: Hope

Hannah, too, had reason to laugh, first in sorrow, then in joy. Her song in 1 Samuel 2 is a declaration of reversal. The barren woman bears children. The hungry are fed. The lowly are lifted. This is hope that surprises. It turns the world upside down, not through brute force, but through unexpected grace.

In Galatians, Paul pleads with the church to remember what first awakened their faith. He is heartbroken, not because they have grown, but because they have regressed—trading the freedom of grace for the slavery of law. He says, "Have I now become your enemy by telling you the truth?" Sometimes the surprise of hope is that it looks like a challenge, a call to return to love.

Advent hope catches us off guard. It shows up when we least expect it and offers more than we dared to ask for. It reminds us that God's timeline is not ours, and neither is God's grace. It is never too late for hope to break in.

Prayer

God of surprise, help me not to laugh off your promises. Let me receive your hope even when it feels too good to be true. Make me ready for your grace, even if it catches me off guard. Amen.

And may that surprising hope be the joy you didn't know you were missing.

Day 3

Hope That Breaks Through

Texts: 1 Samuel 2:1–10;
Genesis 21:1–21; Galatians 4:21—5:1

HOPE DOES NOT ALWAYS wait quietly. Sometimes, it kicks down the door. Sometimes, it cries out in a wilderness or a delivery room or a moment of collapse. When Sarah finally holds her child, the child of promise, it is laughter that fills the room, laughter that still carries a hint of mockery, disbelief, even absurdity. And yet, beneath it all, wonder breaks through. "God has brought laughter for me," she says. "Everyone who hears will laugh with me." But not everyone laughs. Hagar is cast out, alone with her son and no more than a skin of water. Even in the joy of fulfillment, there is sorrow, tension, and risk. Yet, even there, hope breaks through. God hears the boy crying. God opens Hagar's eyes. A well appears. Life springs up in a place of abandonment. The promise of Isaac does not cancel Ishmael. God sees them both.

In 1 Samuel, Hannah's song bursts with the same energy. It is not meek or quiet. It is a defiant anthem from someone who knows what it is to be forgotten and finally remembered. "The Lord raises up the poor . . . lifts the needy from the ash heap." Hope overturns things. It upsets power, humbles pride, and fills empty arms with life.

Week Four: Hope

Paul, in Galatians, uses Sarah and Hagar to say something radical. We are not children of slavery, he insists, but children of promise. We are not stuck in what has been. We are free. Free to live, to love, to hope, because Christ has come.

Advent hope does not wait for ideal conditions. It breaks through, sometimes with laughter, sometimes with tears, sometimes with both. It is already here, stirring, arriving, breaking chains and planting seeds. It reminds us that the waiting is not in vain. The story is not over. And the promise still stands.

Prayer

God who sees, when I feel overlooked, remind me that your promises are for me too. Break through my fear and my silence. Let your hope surprise me again. Amen.

And may that hope meet you today, not just in what is coming, but in what is already here.

Day 4

The Disruption of Belonging

Texts: Psalm 80:1–7, 17–19; Genesis 37:2–11; Matthew 1:1–17

WHEN I WAS YOUNGER, my family used to gather and watch a string of family sitcoms, such as *Full House*, *Family Matters*, and *Step by Step*, just to name a few. Each show had its share of conflict, but everything always managed to work out. Problems were resolved in under thirty minutes, usually with a hug and a heartfelt lesson. When we think or hear about "family values," it's easy to compare ourselves to those glossy TV moments, or to the filtered snapshots we scroll through on social media. But real families don't always resolve things by the end of the episode.

Rarely do we see the jagged, imperfect, and beautiful reality of family.

Matthew's genealogy doesn't sanitize the story. It disrupts it. It begins with Abraham, winds through scandal, tragedy, and exile, and lands with Joseph, a man caught in a situation he didn't ask for. This list of names includes outsiders and sinners, kings and nobodies. It's not a highlight reel, it's real life. And that's exactly where Jesus enters.

Joseph, the dreamer in Genesis, finds himself rejected by his brothers, not because of what he did wrong, but because of who he was becoming. The very people meant to protect him betrayed him. Still, God's hand was never absent. Through the betrayal, God was building a story of redemption.

Psalm 80 is the cry of people who feel forgotten. "Restore us, O God," they plead. They feel cut off from belonging—from the family of God. Yet even in that ache, there is trust. Trust that God still sees. Trust that God is not finished.

Advent reminds us that our families may be fractured. Our stories may be complicated. But the story of Jesus includes stories like ours. God chooses to come not through a perfect bloodline but through a broken one. And that gives us hope, because it means there's room in the story for us too.

Prayer

God of tangled family trees and unfinished stories, thank you for not waiting until we had it all together. Remind me that I belong, not because of what I've done, but because of who you are. Amen.

May you rest in the grace that says you are already part of the story, and that God knows how to work with the mess.

Day 5

Hope That Moves Us Forward

Texts: Psalm 89:1–4, 19–26; 2 Samuel 6:1–11; Hebrews 1:1–4

SOMETIMES HOPE DOESN'T FEEL like a bright light or a soaring song. Sometimes, it feels more like movement—small, hesitant steps forward, even when you're unsure what comes next.

David had grand intentions. He gathered thirty thousand men to bring the ark of God to Jerusalem. It was meant to be a triumphant journey, full of joy and celebration. But when Uzzah reached out and touched the ark and was struck down, everything came to a halt. What started with excitement ended in confusion and fear. David paused the journey, left the ark behind, and withdrew.

And yet, that wasn't the end. Three months later, David tried again. This time with humility, reverence, and rejoicing. The hope wasn't gone, it just needed time to grow.

Psalm 89 reminds us why we keep going. "I have made a covenant with my chosen one," God declares. The psalmist holds on to the promise, even when things look uncertain. That's what hope does. It doesn't deny the pain, but it refuses to believe that pain has the last word.

Hebrews speaks of a God who once spoke through prophets, but now speaks through a Son. Jesus is the radiance of God's glory,

Week Four: Hope

the imprint of God's being. And he enters into the brokenness, not from afar, but from within it. He comes not to keep us stuck in fear but to move us forward.

Advent hope is not always bold or confident. Sometimes, it's quiet. Sometimes, it waits. But eventually, it moves. It tries again. It believes that God's promises are not just for then but for now. Even when we've stumbled, even when we've paused in fear—hope keeps going.

Prayer

God of second chances, when my hope falters, help me try again. Give me courage to move forward, even when I feel unsure. Let your covenant promise carry me through every pause, every setback, every step. Amen.

Today, may you step forward in hope, knowing that God walks with you—even when you don't yet see the way.

Day 6

Hope That Comes Home

Texts: Psalm 89:1–4, 19–26; 2 Samuel 6:12–19; Hebrews 1:5–14

SOMETIMES WE FORGET THAT joy can be messy. That celebration often comes after failure. That hope, when it finally breaks through, doesn't always look polished or polite.

David knew what it was to try and fail. His first attempt to bring the ark of the covenant to Jerusalem ended in tragedy. But now, after time and reflection, he tries again. This time, he doesn't lead with prestige or protocol. He leads with joy. He strips off his royal robe, forgets about appearances, and dances in the streets. Some found it inappropriate. Undignified. But for David, this was worship. It was hope embodied.

Hope will make you move like that sometimes. It will loosen your grip on decorum. It will pull you toward something better, even when the past has wounded you. David had every reason to stay guarded. But instead, he throws a feast and blesses the people. His hope isn't timid. It's public.

Generous.

Alive.

Psalm 89 echoes this covenant joy. The psalmist sings of God's faithfulness across generations, of promises made and promises

Week Four: Hope

kept. "I have found my servant David," the Lord says, "and with my holy oil I have anointed him." It's not just about David's kingship. It's about the God who refuses to forget what love began. The God who stays.

Hebrews turns our eyes from David to a greater king. Jesus is the fulfillment of all that David could only hint at. He is the radiance of God's glory. The one who makes the invisible visible. His reign is not seasonal or symbolic. It is eternal. And still, this King draws near. Still, he comes close. Still, he brings hope home.

Advent hope is not passive. It shows up in streets, in sanctuaries, in ordinary people who choose to trust again. It throws its arms wide and doesn't care who's watching. It brings joy where sorrow used to live. It turns failure into feasting. It reminds us that God's promises are not just for someday. They are for now.

Prayer

God who comes home to us, teach me to dance again. Let my joy be louder than my fear, and my hope deeper than my doubt. Remind me that your promises do not expire. Amen.

Today, may you welcome hope as a guest who brings laughter, healing, and maybe even a little dancing.

Day 7

Hope That Breaks the Silence

Texts: Psalm 89:1–4, 19–26; 2 Samuel 7:1–17; Luke 1:67–80

SOMETIMES, THE SILENCE LASTS longer than we expected. Promises feel delayed. Prayers go unanswered. And we start to wonder if God is still listening at all. Advent is honest about that. It names the silence. It doesn't pretend the waiting is easy.

Zechariah knew something about silence. He had gone mute after questioning the angel's promise. But now, the child is born, and his voice returns—not in complaint but in praise. Luke 1 tells us his first words were a prophecy, a song that burst forth after months of holding back. His son John would prepare the way. But even more, this child would be a sign that God still keeps promises.

The psalmist declares, "I will sing of your steadfast love, O Lord, forever." But it's not always easy to sing. That's why Zechariah's song matters. It reminds us that even after long silence, worship can still rise. That God has not forgotten. That hope isn't gone, only gathering strength.

In 2 Samuel, David wants to build God a house. But God flips the plan. Instead of accepting David's offer, God promises to build him a house—a lineage, a covenant, a future. It's not the kind of hope David expected. It's better. It's lasting. It's grace.

Week Four: Hope

Hope doesn't always look like answered prayers or perfect plans. Sometimes, it looks like an old man singing in surprise. Sometimes it sounds like a whisper in the dark. But it always begins with God. Not with what we do for God, but what God has done—and is still doing—for us.

Advent hope isn't just a candle. It's a voice that breaks the silence. It's a song when we didn't think we had anything left to sing. It's a reminder that God's story is still unfolding, and somehow, we're in it.

Prayer

God of hope, when my voice falters and the silence grows long, remind me that you are still writing the story. Fill my mouth with praise, even when the waiting feels heavy. Let your promises give me courage. Amen.

Today, may you find your voice again, and may it carry the song of hope into places still waiting for light.

CHRISTMAS

The Disruption Fulfilled

We have waited, watched, and wondered our way through Advent. We have wrestled with peace, joy, love, and hope, not as tidy answers, but as holy disruptions. Now the day arrives. But Christmas is not a finish line. It is a beginning. The promise has not ended; it has only just begun. God is not done speaking, not done saving, not done surprising us. The Word became flesh, and that changes everything.

Christmas doesn't ignore the pain of the world. It enters it. It doesn't erase the waiting; it fills it with presence. The miracle of the incarnation is not that everything is suddenly perfect but that God has come close. Close enough to touch. Close enough to cry. Close enough to save.

So today, we don't just remember the birth of a baby. We celebrate the arrival of God-with-us—then, now, and still to come.

Christmas Eve (Morning)

The Disruption We Needed

Texts: 1 Samuel 2:1–10; Genesis 37:2–11; Matthew 1:1–17

GOD HAS NEVER CHOSEN the obvious route. From the very beginning, the story of salvation winds through strange paths and broken families. It's easy to skip over genealogies like the one in Matthew 1, but if you read closely, you'll see a messy line of people with scandal, sorrow, and surprise in their stories. It's not a highlight reel; it's a grace reel. And somehow, God uses every one of them to lead to Jesus.

Joseph, in Genesis, was a dreamer. His dreams got him in trouble, even with his own family. But what looked like betrayal and dysfunction was actually the beginning of redemption. God was already weaving hope through jealousy and rejection. Disruption was not the end—it was the way.

Hannah's prayer in 1 Samuel is a song of reversal. The proud brought low. The lowly lifted up. The hungry fed. The barren filled. It sounds a lot like Mary's song. It is the language of Advent. It's what God does—interrupts, upends, transforms.

This is the disruption we needed: a Savior who does not wait for perfect conditions but enters the middle of the mess. A story that does not erase the past but redeems it. The morning of

Christmas: The Disruption Fulfilled

Christmas Eve reminds us that God has been setting this table for a long time. Every broken piece was never beyond God's reach. Every story, even ours, can be drawn into grace.

Prayer

God of every generation, thank you for showing up in unlikely places. When my story feels too broken or too complicated, remind me that you are still writing it. Use even the hard parts for something holy. Amen.

And may that grace disrupt what you thought was too far gone and make it part of the story of hope.

Christmas Eve (Nativity)

The Disruption That Changed Everything

Texts: Isaiah 9:2–7; Psalm 96; Titus 2:11–14; Luke 2:1–14 [15–20]

CHRIST IS BORN, NOT in power, but in vulnerability. Not in a palace, but in a stable. Not to royalty, but to an unwed mother and a bewildered fiancé. This is how God chose to come. Not with spectacle, but with flesh and crying and mess. And it changed everything.

The world of Luke's Gospel is dominated by Rome. Power moves from palaces, emperors, and decrees. Yet, as Caesar issues commands, heaven breaks open in a shepherd's field. Angels proclaim glory, not to the elite, but to the ordinary. Isaiah's prophecy thunders through the centuries: "The people who walked in darkness have seen a great light." That light is now wrapped in cloth and lying in a manger.

This is not how the world expected salvation. But it is how God works, disrupting the expected, upending our assumptions. God comes in peace, not conquest. In humility, not pride. In grace, not fear.

Titus affirms it: "The grace of God has appeared, bringing salvation to all." That grace has a name. His name is Jesus. And

Christmas: The Disruption Fulfilled

tonight, we celebrate the truth that grace is not a theory, not a doctrine, not a dream. Grace has appeared. Grace has a face.

This is the disruption that changed everything. God with us. Light in the darkness. Joy that will not be silenced.

Prayer

God of incarnation, thank you for entering our world, not with might, but with mercy. Let your grace appear again tonight in our hearts, our homes, and our hurting world. Amen.

And may that grace hold you, even in the quiet hours of the night.

Christmas Day

The Kind of God Who Came Close

John 1:1–14

WE OFTEN ASK BIG questions at Christmas, questions about meaning, about faith, about the kind of world we live in. But the most important question might be this: What kind of God would come like this?

What kind of God would come as a baby, fragile and crying, instead of a thunderous king? What kind of God would trade majesty for a manger? Would draw near, not with spectacle, but with skin?

This God doesn't wait for the world to come to him. He comes to us. He chooses ordinary people—shepherds, young women, fishermen, sinners. He welcomes the broken, eats with the outcast, and touches the untouchable. This God calms storms, heals wounds, tells stories, and washes feet. And he keeps showing up in unexpected places.

Christmas tells us what kind of God we have. A God who draws near. A God who wraps himself in flesh. A God who doesn't stay far off but pitches a tent in the middle of our chaos. In Jesus, God becomes tangible. Touchable. Knowable.

Christmas: The Disruption Fulfilled

Look into the eyes of a newborn child, and you'll see it—the mystery of Christmas. This is not a God who hides but a God who comes close.

Prayer

God-with-us, remind us that you have not stayed distant. You have drawn near. You came in weakness to show strength, in love to overcome fear. Help us see you—not just in the nativity scene but in the everyday. Amen.

And may that love keep drawing near, until the whole world knows what kind of God we serve.

Closing Reflection
Disrupted, Reoriented, Sent

ADVENT ENDS, BUT DISRUPTION never really does. At least, not the kind that comes from God. The arrival of Christ does not simply wrap things up with a bow. It turns the world upside down—or perhaps right side up. The child born in a borrowed stable is not the end of the story but the beginning of a whole new creation. Immanuel, God with us, means that nothing can ever be quite the same again.

Throughout these weeks, we've reflected on peace, joy, love, and hope. These themes aren't just seasonal sentiments; they are meant to shape how we live. They are not confined to sanctuaries or songs but are meant to spill out into our homes, our streets, and our broken and beautiful world. Advent teaches us to wait, but not passively. We wait like people leaning forward, alert and ready for the sound of footsteps. And now the footsteps have come. God has arrived—not in splendor but in vulnerability. Not above us but among us.

I can think of all the times my life has been disrupted, some moments welcome, others painful. I've had disruptions that knocked the breath out of me, and others that opened my eyes to joy I didn't know I needed. But in hindsight, many of those disruptions were holy. They reoriented me. They shaped me. They made room for something deeper than comfort—something like grace.

So where do we go from here?

Closing Reflection

We carry Advent with us. We carry it into boardrooms and back porches, into classrooms and shelters and checkout lines. We carry it into conversations that are hard and neighborhoods that are hurting. The world doesn't stop needing hope just because the calendar says December 25. Our longing for peace doesn't fade just because the season is over.

The truth is, God is still disrupting. Still calling. Still drawing near. Christ has come, and Christ will come again—but in the meantime, we live like people who have seen the light. Not because we always feel it. Not because life is suddenly easy. But because Advent formed us to expect God in the unexpected, to trust that even in the silence, something holy is being born.

So, may the Christ who disrupted everything, disrupt you too—your routines, your fears, your cynicism. May he unsettle the parts of you that have settled for less. And may his light guide your feet into the kind of life that looks more like him: humble, courageous, interruptible, and full of grace.

And when the music fades and the lights come down, may you remember: Advent was never just a season. It is a way of seeing. A way of walking. A way of being ready—for God is not finished. The story is just beginning.

Finally, may you see each disruption as a holy disruption, revealing how God is still writing your story.

www.ingramcontent.com/pod-product-compliance
Lightning Source LLC
Chambersburg PA
CBHW071732040426
42446CB00011B/2331